Forex for Beginners

How to Make Money Trading Global
Currency Markets

Table of Contents

Introduction

I want to thank you for purchasing the book, "Forex for Beginners, How to Make Money Trading Global Currency Markets".

This book contains proven steps and strategies on how to analyze and trade currencies.

Have you ever dreamt of being your own boss, of being able to work the hours that you want to work? Hours that best suits your lifestyle and personal commitments? Being able to book a holiday without having to seek approval from your superiors?

Well the great news is that with some commitment, an internet connection, and a laptop, you can make these dreams a reality. Let's get one thing straight, this book isn't a get rich quick scheme that promises to make you a millionaire overnight. If that's what you're looking for then this book isn't for you.

What this book aims to do is provide you with the basic knowledge and steps that can enable you to build the blocks that will give you a greater chance of succeeding. After reading this book you will be able to enter the market with a greater degree of confidence than if you entered without it.

So if you are looking for a career change or even just a new thrilling hobby then this book can guide you into making the correct decisions and choices.

More and more people are getting worried about what their financial future may hold. They are scared of being left without any resources at the time of retirement. People are fed up with working for somebody else and want to start their own businesses. A lot of us are searching for ways to make more than we spend. With the internet, new technologies, and financial markets that are available to anyone this has become more than achievable.

There are a lot of ways how to achieve above mentioned targets and investing is one of them. Lots of people tend to go to the stock market and they use the only strategy they know of: buy and hold. Fortunately, there is more than one way to make money in the financial markets. This book will show you a number of trading systems that will help you to trade the largest financial market in the world and actually make some money.

Thanks again for purchasing this book, I hope you enjoy it

What is Forex trading?

Forex (short for foreign exchange) is the largest financial market in the world where investors, speculators and traders trade currencies for profit. The market was initially created to satisfy a demand for various currencies in trade between countries of the world who were doing business together. However, with time the market became a place where most of transactions took place with the expectation to make profit on currency fluctuations rather than the exchange of one currency to another for international business purposes. Statistics show that around ninety percent of the daily transactions in the Forex market have a speculative character as market participants hope to make money by speculating on the direction of various currency pairs for that specific day, week, month, or even year.

Transactions of currencies take place between two parties, usually over an electronic network or in case of large orders currencies can also be traded over the telephone. Conversely to various Stock Exchanges currency markets are not centralized, meaning that currencies can be traded anywhere in the world and are open twenty four hours per day and almost six days per week. On an average day anywhere from 2 to 4 trillion US dollars change hands in the market. No wonder it is the most attractive market for traders!

Currency pairs
If you open a Forex chart you will see such symbols as: eur/usd, gbp/usd, usd/jpy or eur/gbp. These mean that currencies are paired and are not traded separately. You may

also hear such terms as "base currency" or "quote currency". The first currency is always "base currency" and the second one is always the "quote currency". So, if you see gbp/usd in your chart, you are looking at British Pound/United States Dollar currency pair. At the time of writing gbp/usd quote is 1.4650. It means that you need to pay that amount of dollars to get 1 British Pound.

If you trade gbp/usd you can buy it or even sell it. By buying Pounds you automatically sell US dollars and by selling US dollars you automatically buy British Pounds.

Below is the table with major currencies. All of them can be traded against one another in pairs.

Major currencies

Symbol	Country	Currency	Nickname(s)
USD	United States	US Dollar	Buck, Greenback
EUR	Euro zone members	Euro	Fiber
JPY	Japan	Japanese Yen	Yen
GBP	Great Britain	British Pound	Cable
CHF	Switzerland	Swiss Franc	Swissy
CAD	Canada	Canadian Dollar	Loonie
AUD	Australia	Australian Dollar	Aussie
NZD	New Zealand	New Zealand Dollar	Kiwi

The pairs that do not have US dollar in a pair are called currency crosses. The most popular currency crosses are: eur/jpy, eur/aud, gbp/jpy, gbp/chf and gbp/aud.

Spreads and pips

If you open any platform and look at the quotes of currency pairs you will see that there is a difference between the bid and ask prices (bid price is a buy price of base currency and ask is a sell price of base currency). My given example of gbp/usd pair at the time of writing would be **1.4650/1.4652**. You can see that the difference between the bid and ask price is two points or as it is known in Forex: 2 pips. A pip is the smallest amount that a pair can move either direction in a pair. The difference between buy and sell prices is called a spread. Any currency pair that your broker quotes will have a spread and it will vary depending on a currency pair. Major pairs will usually have 1-4 pip spreads, while currency crosses or more exotic currencies may have 4-40 pip spreads. So, if you open, let's say a buy position in gbp/usd, when your order is opened on your platform you will see that you have a floating loss of two pips. If price moves in your direction, this loss will become profit. Brokers are compensated by means of spreads.

Leverage in Forex

Forex is very attractive to market players, because you can use big leverage while trading currencies. Leverage is like a loan that you get from your broker or a bank and you can operate much bigger amount of money while trading than you really have. In Forex you can use 1:50 or even 1:1000 leverage. It means that for your every dollar leverage provider can give from 50 to 1000 dollars more to trade. So, if you open a mini account with 100 US dollar and with a leverage of 1:100, you can actually operate 10 000 US dollar position. This increases your chances to make big money, but also your risk. You need to be careful using leverage and try to avoid risking more than 5 percent of your deposit on any given trade.

Market players

As the currency market is very big it abounds in players that play it. Some leave a huge impact on it and some are not that important at all. Central banks and governments are the ones you want to be aware of. If interest rates are raised or some government implements laws that are going to have impact on the exchange rates you can be sure that market will react to these moves. Central banks and governments can intervene in Forex in order to change direction of some specific currencies or slow the move for some time. Commercial banks and mega financial institutions also leave a trail when they enter the market. These play with billions of dollars and no wonder they impact exchange rates. Hedgers and commercial traders are mostly busy with international trade and trade the market in order to hedge their positions. Hedge funds, investment funds and big speculators also trade the market with expectations to make profits. Some of them are long term investors; others simply keep positions for a few weeks and yet others a few days or a few hours. Individual traders like you and me do not impact the market as our amounts of money are too small to change the rates.

Types of orders

There is more than just one way to enter your trade. All Forex brokers are supposed to offer you the ones that we will discuss briefly here.

Market orders

This is the type of order that allows you to buy or sell a currency pair at a current price. So, if you want to trade gbp/usd that is currently quoted **1.4650/1.4652** you would be buying it at 1.4650 and selling at 1.4652.

Limit orders

Limit orders can be of two types: *limit buy* and *limit sell*.

You place *limit buy* orders below current market price and they are executed only when the price falls to that level.

You place *limit sell* orders above current market price and they are executed only when the price rises to that level.

Stop orders

Stop orders are also of two types: *buy stop* and *sell stop*.

You place *buy stop* orders above the current price and they are executed when price reaches that level.

You place *sell stop* orders below the current price and they are executed only when price reaches that level.

Stop loss orders

Risk control is very important in trading currencies. You need to decide how much you are going to risk per trade before you enter it. Stop loss order will automatically close your open trade at a predefined level and help you to prevent further losses.

Take profit orders

Take profit order will close your trade at a predefined level if price goes in the direction you anticipated. When that level is reached, your trade will be automatically closed.

Trailing stop order

Trailing stop order is order that let's your position move together with the price. It works both as *stop loss* and a *take profit* order. If you have a certain number of pips of profit you can trail your stop as price continues to move in your anticipated direction. If price moves by a certain number of pips against you (you define how many) your position is automatically closed.

Forex trading sessions

It has already been said that FX market is open 24 hours a day five days per week. It is very good as you can trade the market any time of the day depending on where you live. Market trading hours are traditionally divided into three sessions.

Asian session

FX market opens on Sunday when Asian session starts. The main countries that fall within the zone are: Japan, China, Australia, New Zealand and Russia. Tokyo is the main financial centre for Asian session. Volatility is pretty low during this session.

European session

When the Asian session comes to an end, the European session starts. The main countries that are within the zone are: Germany, France, and other big European countries, but the main financial centre for the European session is London. The largest number of transactions takes place when the London market opens.

North American session

European session merges with North American session. When the New York market opens the European session is not over yet and you may see a lot of volatility during the New York open. The main countries that are within the zone are: Canada, Mexico and some big South American countries too. The centre for the session is New York.

Types of market analysis

The forex market can be analyzed in a number of ways, but the main methods are: **fundamental analysis** and **technical analysis**.

Fundamental analysis has various economic and macroeconomic indicators at its core for predicting the future direction of exchange rates. The main indicators are: interest rates, inflation, unemployment figures, general domestic product and retail sales.

Those who look at the market using technical analysis tend to study past prices and then predict future price moves. They have a lot of technical indicators in their arsenal such as: Stochastic, moving averages or overbought/oversold indicators. Other try to analyze support and resistance levels and yet others look for trend continuation or reversal patterns such as: head and shoulders, triple/double top, triangles, pennants, flags, diamonds, etc... Don't worry about these strange terms, it's something you will come across and study about at a later point.

Forex versus Other Markets

When people get interested in investing they usually select the most conservative option, the only one they are aware of and that is investing in stocks. It is good and you probably have heard a lot of success stories how such and such made a killing in the US Stock market. Others are even more conservative and they just invest in government bonds simply expecting to get a small return on their investment, not to make a fortune. Unfortunately, most aspiring investors neglect one of the biggest opportunities - investing in the global currency market. I want to outline the advantages of the market over other financial markets below.

One of the biggest advantages is to use high leverage in trading currencies. It has already been mentioned that you can use from 5:1 to 100:1 or even 1000:1 with some brokers. In some stock markets around the world you will not be able to use leverage at all. With some US Stock markets the highest leverage you can get is 3:1.

Another benefit of Forex is that it is open 24 hours per day, which cannot be said about stock or other financial markets. If you intend to be a trader you will find out that Forex has different levels of volatility during different market hours and you are free to choose which hours you want to trade which helps enormously when learning how to trade alongside a full time job.

There are no shorting (selling) rules in the currency market. Shorting is borrowing an asset to sell it without buying it first. This is a practice that a lot of professionals use. Markets are in different states at different times and when a bear (downtrend) market starts shorting (selling), a security is the best choice to take. This is not a problem with Forex as all currencies are paired and by buying one currency you automatically sell (short) another. So, you can trade bear markets as easily as you can trade the bullish ones. In some other markets you may need to wait an uptick before you can short a security and in others you do not have this possibility at all.

Forex also does not have any limiting rules for day trading. You can open a position today and close it the same day. In fact, with most brokers you can open an order and close it in a matter of seconds without any problems. Furthermore, you can open a multitude of positions and close them in a few minutes, or again seconds. Some traders, who use a scalping trading strategy, do it every day by opening and closing hundreds of position in 24 hour period.

Most professional traders use various types of orders to trade currencies: stop loss, limit orders, buy stop, sell stop, trailing stops and etc. These options are usually available with most Forex brokers. You will hardly find those in other markets even with the best brokers.

The forex industry can boast the smallest fees in the financial markets. In a sense, there are actually no fees. Forex brokers are compensated by means of spreads that are very low at the moment. Some brokers can actually quote eur/usd pair with 0.4 pip spread. Of course, other pairs have bigger spreads, but that is by far better choice than paying a fixed fee for opening a position in stocks or other securities. Apart from the spreads most FX brokers do not take any extra fees.

Anyone starting a bank with as little as 100$ can open a mini account with most Forex brokers. Standard accounts can be opened with a minimum amount of 2000$. In comparison to other financial markets these are very small sums. So, if you want to start investing in currencies you do not need thousands of dollars to start with, you can begin with hundreds and then proceed on to bigger amounts if you are successful. Another option that many brokers offer is a practice account. You can start trading the real time markets with a virtual play fund of typically $50,000. This is a great way to get started as you are risking nothing in order to gain valuable experience for no risk at all to your money.

Basic Forex trading strategies

If you start a business you have to know what you are doing. It is foolish just to start a company without a plan and expect that everything will turn out somehow and money will start rolling over to your bank account. No sound businessman thinks that way. Good investors and speculators do not think that way either. They study financial markets for years and develop their own systems. Now, this may sound disappointing, but it shouldn't. Successful traders have been trading markets for centuries and a lot of their strategies have been described in books. You see, markets do not change, because people do not change. The same things that worked a few hundred years ago in the markets will work today. As you become a more proficient trader you will learn how to filter the systems that are described in the chapter and probably create one of your own, but you need to know where you can start. This chapter will introduce you to basic trading strategies that can be applied to any financial market, especially Forex.

Long or short term trading
Firstly, it is important to decide what time horizon you are interested in. We can basically divide traders into three groups: long term, intermediate and short term traders. Long term traders usually trade long term market trends and they can be called trend traders. Intermediate term traders wait for

market swings that typically last from a few days to a few weeks; maximum a month and they are usually called swing or range traders. Short term traders try to capitalize on daily fluctuations in currencies and usually open and close trades within 24 hours. These are usually called day traders. Let us look through the basic strategies that these traders use.

Trend trading

Trend trading is probably the most famous trading strategy that has been used by investors for hundreds of years. It is mostly considered a long term strategy, but some traders wait for short term trends that may last from a few hours to a few days. Anyway, a trend is a tendency in currencies that causes a currency pair to go in one direction for a protracted period of time.

There has to be some fundamental factors for a trend to start and last. Trends do not happen too often and currencies stay within confined ranges for a long period of time before a tendency develops. Statistics shows that any given currency pair would spend about 2 months in a trend and around 10 months in a range in any given year.

How does a trend start?

It has been said that currencies spend much of the time in ranges. They fluctuate between the high and the low of the range. Eventually, some event causes prices to go out of the range and we can state that it is the moment when a trend starts. **When currency pair leaves its' previous range a trend starts.**

How do we trade a trend?

One of the best way to trade a trend is to open a position at the moment when a currency pair leaves its' previous range. A picture tells a thousand words. Below is a chart of usd/jpy (US dollar/Japanese Yen) pair. We can see that from the April of 2011 to December of 2012 the pair stayed in a range between 75.50 and 85.50 levels. That is the range of about 1000 pips. Of course, for most of the time price was contained in even smaller ranges. However, 85.50 was the top of the range and 75.50 was the low of the range. You can see what happened when that range was eventually broken. A trend started and prices rallied upwards for half a year.

So, one had to wait when the price broke the top of the range of 85.50 by some 10 pips and enter a buy order. We talked about types of orders in our first chapter. You simply had to place a buy stop order at around 85.60 level (with a 100 pip stop loss order in case market turned against you) and leave it there. When price reached the level your order would have been filled and you would be riding a trend and making thousands of pips.

Chart no 1. usd/jpy weekly chart

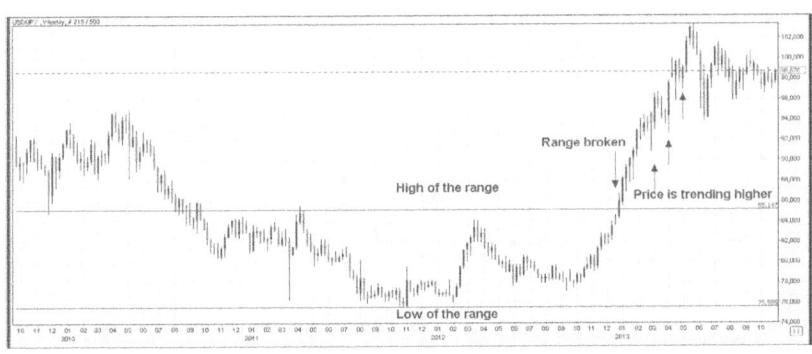

15

An opposite example happened with aud/usd (Australian dollar/US dollar) pair. The pair was stuck in a range from April of 2014 to September of 2014. The high of the range was 0.9500 and the low of the range was 0.9200. It was a pretty narrow range of only 300 pips. Look what happened when the range was broken. A downtrend started that caused the pair to drop for about 1500 pips.

You could have traded the move by simply placing a sell stop order (read the first chapter about types of orders) below the low of the range (10 pips below it) at about 0.9190 level and leave it there (with a 100 pip stop loss order in case market turned against you). When price started going down your order would have been opened and you would have made tremendous amounts of pips.

Chart no 2. aud/usd daily chart

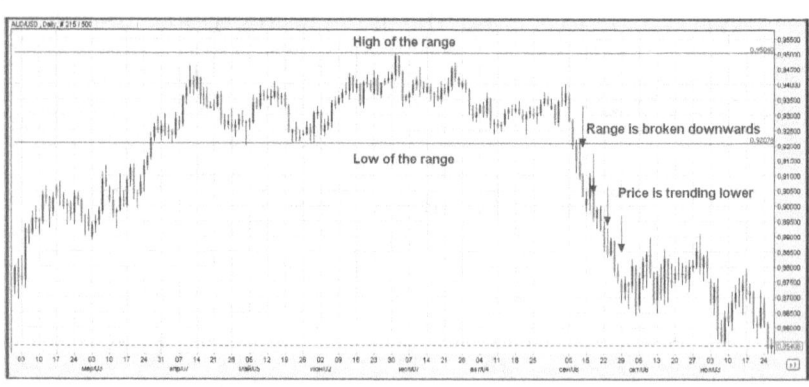

These two examples show that you can trade big market trends in both directions up and down and make a lot of pips.

Range/swing trading

Another common trading strategy is range/swing trading. We know that most of the time currencies stay in ranges and do not really trend. If 10 out 12 months they are ranging it is wise to find out how you can capitalize on that and not simply wait for a trend to start.

After a market stops trending it usually starts ranging and forms the high and the low of a range. It then stays within that range for a prolonged period of time before new information reaches the market, a new trend starts and price goes beyond the limits of the range. You simply have to see whether new highs in an uptrend or new lows in a downtrend are no longer made and then you can safely state that a trend is over and time for range/swing trading has come.

When this period comes a price will usually fluctuate between the high and the low of the range presenting traders an opportunity to buy at the bottom of the range (support) and to sell at the top of the range (resistance).

There is hardly ever an ideal situation when price comes back at exactly the top of the bottom of the range. It may fall short some 30-60 pips and then swings back. The basic of idea of trading this strategy is to wait for some signs or reversal at the top and bottom. **Price has to stop rising at the top of the range and falling at the bottom of the range.** In most cases it reverses within 24 hours when it reaches those extreme points of a range and heads back in the opposite direction. You can also see bearish candles at the top and bullish at the bottom. These are signs that prices are about to reverse and you need to take action. Candles are the names given to the time frames of a price action and is illustrated on the chart below. Don't worry too much about candle patterns at this stage. Just try and understand what is happening to the price.

Chart no 3. usd/cad 8 hour chart

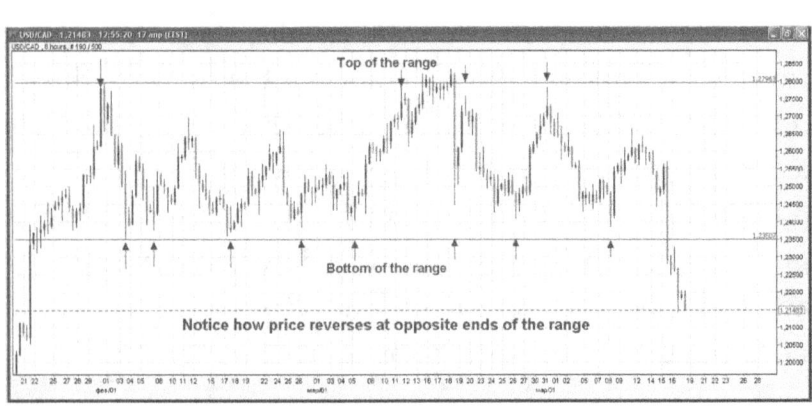

How to trade a range

Just look at the 8 hour chart of usd/cad (US dollar/Canadian dollar). You can see that from beginning of February 2015 till April 15 of 2015 it has been in a range 1.2350-1.2800 (450 pip range).

It is obvious that 1.2350-1.2400 level acted as support. Price stopped from falling having reached the level. You could trade it by simply buying usd/cad pair around 1.2410 level with a 80 pip stop loss order at 1.2330 level and take profit 1.2650 (240 pip profit). During this period you would have had at least 5 profitable trades and 1 unprofitable (when range ended and price broke down).

In the same fashion it is easy to spot that 1.2750-1.2800 level acted as resistance. You could trade it by selling usd/cad pair at 1.2740 with a stop loss of 80 pips at 1.2820 and take profit at 1.2460 (280 pip profit). One trade would have been closed with a loss and two with a profit.

Breakout trading strategy

There are a lot of day trading strategies and they require a lot of time and skill to master. Therefore, we decided to describe the last trading strategy that is often used by professional traders and in terms of time horizon it can be used on a short term, intermediate and even long term basis.

In order for a breakout to occur there has to be some sort of range. Again, time period is not important. The idea of breakout trading is that the longer price stays within a range, the stronger the pressure becomes for that security to come out of the range. When highs and lows of a range are made, the range tends to get more and more narrow until finally the price has to breakout. Breakout traders take advantage of the momentum that is created when price moves out that range. A lot of traders tend to place buy and stop orders beyond the limits of a given range. Finally, when those limits are breached the price simply explodes in that direction due to large number of orders being filled. This momentum price movement continues for some time till it finally fades.

This strategy works particularly well when a currency pair has moved for a prolonged period of time and then took a breather. It then fluctuates for a few days or a week within a narrowing range and when the pressure becomes too strong and range too narrow a breakout occurs.

19

Below you can see an example of a breakout trade in eur/usd pair.

Chart no 5. eur/usd 2 hour chart

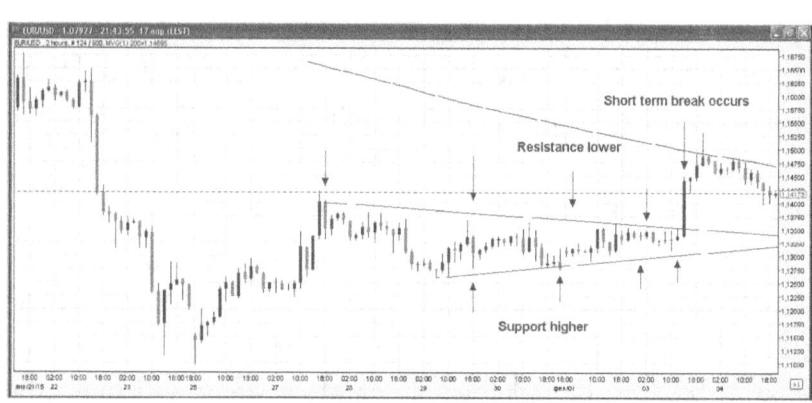

How to trade a breakout

From the 27th of January to the 3rd of February 2015 eur/usd pair was in a narrowing range after it bounced from its current downtrend. Bull and bear power was in equilibrium, because selling pressure would become lower and buying pressure higher. Finally, on the 3rd of February the price had to go either way and it went upwards.

In this type of situations you can simply place a buy stop order above the most recent high and a sell stop order below the most recent low.

You can see that on the 2nd of February the range of eur/usd pair was as narrow as 50 pips (pretty small for the pair). The way to trade it was to place a buy stop five pips above 1.1350 with a stop loss below the low 1.1300 (50 pips) and a sell stop five pips below 1.1300 level with a stop loss above the high of the range (50 pips).

In this situation we see that the price broke upwards, which means our buy stop order was triggered and the pair rallied by more than 150 pips. What did you have to do with the other order (sell stop)? You simply had to remove it.

This type of trading strategy removes guessing from your trading as you are ready to go either direction the price will go and you have orders at both ends of a range. You do not have to worry where the price will go. When one of your orders (in either side of the range) is triggered you simply remove the other order and go with the momentum that is caused by a price breakout.

Basic chart patterns

Chart patterns are another field of technical analysis. We know that investors buy and sell currencies and other securities for thousands of reasons. Some do it due to fundamental analysis, others on recommendations, some people follow their hunches and emotions, traders take profits or decide to cut their losses short. When all buyers and sellers put their money at stake this represents eternal economic principles of supply and demand. Ultimately, whichever of the two dominates, that will be reflected in price action and the price will either continue in the direction it has been going or reverse. Before the price change happens this is often reflected in the price by means of formation of chart patterns that are a graphical expression of supply and demand. When demand dominates prices rise and when supply does, prices fall.

Therefore, chart patterns are divided into two groups: continuation and reversal. If a trend stops and starts showing some signs of reversal we often see a reversal pattern formed. If price stops for a while and then continues trending in its previous direction we often see a continuation pattern formed before the price actually starts moving. You can spot these price patterns on various time frames from minute to monthly charts. Let us look at some basic patterns from both of these groups.

Reversal patterns

Reversal patterns are formed before a change in an ongoing trend happens. Smart traders can use that to close their existing positions that they have opened in the direction of the prevailing trend. They would also look for proper moment to enter the trades in the opposite direction.

Head and shoulders (bearish)/inverted head and shoulders (bullish)

Head and shoulders pattern is often formed at the end of an uptrend and indicates that prices will turn lower if price pattern is validated. The pattern consists of three peaks: left shoulder, head (the highest peak) and right shoulder. Ideally left and right shoulders are similar in size and length.

Left shoulder is the first peak. When the high point of it is reached price often reverses and goes down. Then price rallies again and pushes up by taking away previous high where the second peak (head) is formed. Price collapses again and reaches about the same level of the decline from left shoulder, possibly lower or higher. Price rallies again, but the high of the head is not reached and price starts falling again. This is when the right shoulder is formed. Now the low of the left shoulder and the low of the head form a neckline. If price collapses from the right shoulder through the neckline and continues going down the pattern is validated and we can state that a downtrend started.

How to trade it

Most traders enter a sell stop order right below the neckline. When the neckline is breached your order is opened and you go with the prevailing trend. It is commonly accepted that the minimum target that may be reached after the neckline is broken is the distance from the peak of the head to the neckline. If that distance is about 500 pips we can assume that's how much price will go when the neckline is broken. The chart below will help you understand. So, you can place a take profit order of 500 pips, which is your minimum expected target. You can try for more, but then move your stop loss (trailing as mentioned earlier), so that you could protect your profits.

Below is the example of eur/aud daily chart. The pattern developed in a matter of 4 months. You can see that the pair was in an uptrend before the formation of a pattern. On December 27, 2013 it formed the first peak (left shoulder). It then collapsed and formed the low on the 13th of January 2014. It rallied beyond its' previous peak and formed another peak (the head) on the 24th of January, 2014. It then went down again and made the second low on the 13th of February, 2014. We connect two low points and get the neckline of the pattern. After the second low price soared, but failed to reach previous high, formed right shoulder and then collapsed through the neckline. The distance from head to neckline was about 840 pips and therefore our target for selling eur/aud after the break of the neckline was about 1.4140 level marked (minimum expected target) on the chart. Be sure to use stop loss that is at least four times smaller than your take profit target.

Chart no 6. Head and shoulders pattern

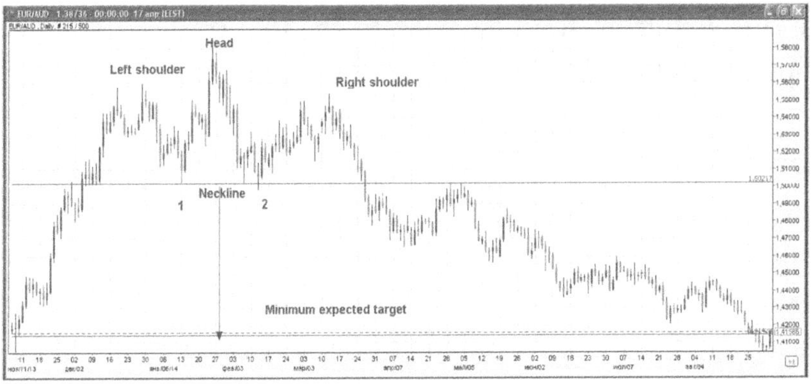

The same is true about a downtrend. When a downtrend ends, an inverted head and shoulders can be formed indicating that a bearish trend is over and a bullish trend is about to start. All the rules for formation are the same, except the pattern is inverted.

Double top (bearish)/double bottom (bullish)

Double top is a bearish reversal pattern found at the end of an uptrend. It consists of two peaks that are basically equal.

So, there must be a prior uptrend for a pattern to form. The first peak should be the highest high of the pattern. After it is reached the price starts falling. After some time, bullish price action follows and the price rallies back to its' previous top, but fails to break it. The second peak is formed. It may be slightly lower or slightly higher than the first peak. Then, the price reverses again and goes back to previous peak low. That should act as support. If support is broken pattern is validated and a downtrend starts.

The minimum expected target for the move down would be the distance from the first peak to the low of the first decline from the first peak.

Most traders would wait for the support to be broken before entering a sell order. That is one of the best ways to trade double top, because we can only know whether it is a double top or not if the support is broken convincingly. So, you can place a sell stop 10-20 pips below support level and if price goes there your order is opened and you can go with the market and make nice cash.

Below is the example of a double top on a weekly chart of eur/usd pair.

You can see that the first peak was reached by the middle of April of 2008. The low and support was made in the second week of May, 2008. The price rallied again and the second peak was made around middle of July, 2008. The price then crashed through support and a huge downtrend started in eur/usd. The distance from the first peak to support was around 740 pips and that was our minimum take profit target, which was easily reached within a period of one month. The price then continued crashing.

Chart no 7. Double top pattern

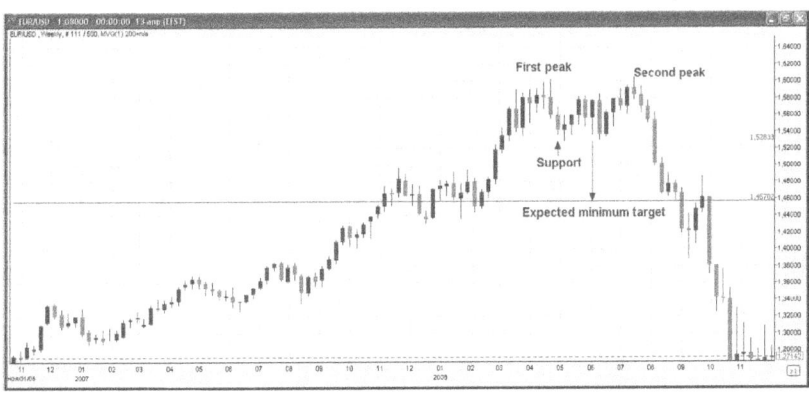

So, you could have entered a sell stop at around 1.5270-60 level with a stop loss of 100 pips and take profit target of 700 pips and eventually enjoyed very nice profit.

The same rules should be applied to double bottom pattern, except inverted.

Continuation patterns

Continuation patterns form when a trend stops for a short while to take a breather and then resumes itself. These patterns tend to be shorter in terms of time and they end up with a breakout strongly in the direction of the previous trends. The best known patterns that belong to the group are: triangles and flags.

Triangles

Triangles are of various types, but they all have the same underlying principle: narrowing range. In order for a pattern to be valid it has to have at least two lower highs and two higher lows (clear indication of a narrowing range). These high and low points can be connected with converging lines (or trend lines) and this gives us a shape of a triangle.

At some point the price has to go through a high or low of the pattern and when that happens we can be sure that the previous trend continues. If the trend was up, we would expect price to go up through the most recent high of a triangle point. If the trend was down, we would expect price to go down through the most recent low of a triangle point.

The target for the possible minimum move after a break is usually calculated by simply measuring the base of a triangle or the highest and lowest points of the triangle. That is the size of an expected move from the breakout point.

Let us look at a triangle that developed in eur/usd downtrend on 8 hour chart. The pattern was pretty short in duration. It lasted from the 8th of August, 2014 to 18th of August, 2014. The base of triangle was around 100 pips and that was our expected minimum target for a break lower. On the 18th of August, the range of the triangle became very narrow and the move lower finally started. 1.3350 levels (the low point numbered 4 on chart) were broken and price easily moved more than 100 pips in two days.

Chart no 8. Bearish triangle

How to trade the pattern?
You could trade the pattern by simply placing a sell stop order below number 4 point of a chart pattern (a buy stop order would be if triangle were bullish and formed after a previous uptrend) with a stop loss of 50 pips and minimum take profit order of 100 pips (double size of a stop loss). When the price reached the level your automatic sell stop order would have been reached and opened and the target reached within a day.

Flags
Flags are also continuation patterns. They usually form when market consolidates after a big move and after a while the trend continues.

A flag must contain a sharp move before consolidation (short term range) starts. This sharp move forms a sort of a flagpole which is a distance from previous point when a move started (support or resistance depending whether trend was up or down) to the current support or resistance point, which is the highest or lowest point of a current flag pattern. Price then forms a short of rectangular sloping channel, which looks like a flag (that's why it is called a flag). If the previous move was up, the sloping channel would be down and if the move was down, the sloping channel would be up. Trend lines will help you to see the slope of a channel and see a flag clearly.

How to trade a flag

Eventually, a bullish flag is broken upwards and price goes through the upper trend line of a channel and a bearish flag is broken downwards as the price goes through the lower trend line of a channel.

So, if you want to trade a bullish flag you need to place a buy stop above the upper trend line of the flag. When the price reaches the level, your order is opened and you can start making some nice pips when price moves in an upward direction. Just be sure to keep your stop tight. It could be around 50 pips.

If you want to trade a bearish flag you need to do everything in reverse. You need to place a sell stop below the lower trend line of the flag. When the price reaches the level, your order is opened and you can make a good amount of pips. Keep your stop loss at around 50 pips.

The most usual way to decide where your take profit target should be is to calculate the size of a flagpole and add that amount of pips to the breakout point.

Below is the example of a bearish flag that developed in a downtrend of eur/usd pair. It took just around a week to form, so it was a really short breather before the downtrend resumed. You can see that the flagpole was around 300 pips in length and when the lower channel trend line was broken the pair easily travelled that distance in one day. You simply had to place a sell stop order at around the 1.1550 level (maybe 10 pips lower) with a 50 pip stop loss and a 300 pip take profit target. The trade would have gone nicely in your favor and you would have made 300 pips of profit. One day's work trading a bearish flag pattern!

Chart no 10. Bearish flag pattern

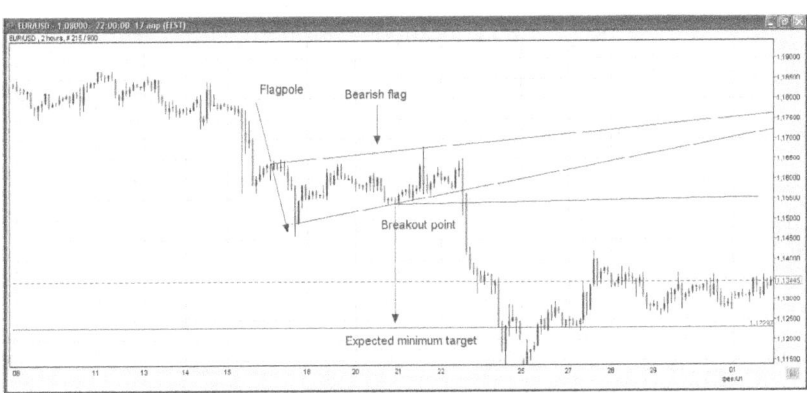

Risk management

When people go on a journey they tend to take a survival kit, the essential things that they might need. It is strange when new aspiring traders expect to succeed somehow without having the essentials of what it takes to be a successful trader. Some key things to succeed in Forex have already been covered in the ebook, but not all. This chapter will deal with one of them. If you have all the rest, but do not have this one, you are going to fail as a trader. This one special thing that will help you to survive and eventually to prosper is risk management.

You have not only to make money, but to protect it.
In most businesses making money and saving money are two things that help you to go on. If you make a lot, but spend even more, you are not really successful and you won't survive as a businessman. Your business will fail. You need to save some of what you make in case something goes wrong.
The same is true with investing with currencies. You not only have to make money to be successful, but you need to protect your capital and what you make if you want to be in the market for the long haul. To start with you should know statistics. Around 80 percent of traders lose all of their invested money in currencies within a year. Most of them, actually, lose it within the first few months of their trading. Why? There are a lot of reasons, but the main is that they risk too much of their capital on trades.

Never risk all of your capital on a single trade

I have heard a lot of stories how traders risked all of their capital on a single trade expecting to make a killing and they actually lost it all. If you expect to do the same, I have a good piece of advice; better go to the casino and play roulette. There is no difference between risking it all on a single trade and gambling at a casino.

You need to protect your capital, because capital is the thing that you are going to make money with. Your money is the tool that helps you to make money. If you push it "all in" and lose, you lose the tool that helps you to make money. You can't afford to be doing that. You need to remember one thing, before you learn how to make money in currencies you have to learn how to protect it.

You also have to remember that you are going to experience good and bad days. You will sometimes experience a "losing streak" when you have a number of trades (in a row) that you are going to close with a loss. If you do not risk much you are going to survive those streaks, if you risk too much you will fail sooner rather than later.

Using a stop loss is not a choice

One of the things that can help you to control your risk is to use a stop loss order. Trading without a stop loss is a sure way to disaster. There are a lot of various fundamental events that happen from time to time and markets start crashing in a matter of seconds. A stop loss maybe the only thing which will help you to survive that!

What is recommended stop loss percentage?
It is clear that if you want to make money you have to risk it. The problem is: how much. Most investors agree that 2 percent of equity is just about the right amount of money that you can risk on a single trade. If you are planning to open a few positions, you still have to be sure that the total risk percentage on all your open trades would not be higher than 2 percent.

Move your stop loss orders when your trade is in profit
Another way to protect your capital and money that you have made is to move your stop loss order when your open trade is in profit. You can never be sure whether your trade will hit your expected profit target. Therefore, when you have a certain amount of pips, it is wise to move your stop loss to the profit zone. Let's say you have 100 pips of profit. You expect price will continue moving further, but you can never be sure. You may move your stop loss order and lock in some profit in case price moves against you. In the example of 100 pip profit you may lock in 50 pips, just to be sure you do not lose everything you have made.

So, I hope you see importance of protecting your capital. Learn this lesson now and it will help you save your capital and possibly your trading career later.

How to choose a Forex broker

Choosing a trustworthy Forex broker is not some unnecessary concern. When I opened my first account about ten years ago I did that through a mega company Refco. It was a well known name at the time. They offered their services for those who wanted to trade various securities, including currencies and options. However, one day the company went bankrupt causing a lot of trouble for its clients. People's accounts and assets were frozen and most of them could not withdraw their money for months. In the end, customers were passed on from Refco to its' daughter company FXCM and so people could get their money back or trade it through FXCM. A recent event in SNB, when the Bank of Switzerland removed the ceiling in eur/chf , caused Swiss Franc to soar thousands of pips in a matter of second. This event also put a lot of brokers in a similar position Refco found itself a decade ago. Some went bankrupt; others may still experience it soon. Knowing that any newbie trader should think carefully what broker he wants to choose. Let us look through some essential things that will help you to choose the most reliable brokers available in the market today.

Do not deal with companies that have had legal issues in the past
You need to be sure whether a company you want to open an account with hasn't had trouble with financial regulators that

deal with the regulation of financial markets. Refco, the company I had already mentioned had to deal with CFTC and NFA (both regulators) on more than one hundred occasions. I did not know that and this cost me money when things eventually unraveled. So, if you want to avoid what I had to go through, better check whether the broker you are interested in is in good standing with these regulators.

Be sure your broker is regulated
You might be surprised, but there are a lot of brokers around that are not really regulated. They simply use some loopholes in their local laws or those brokers are offshore companies that may disappear with your hard earned money any time. Just google "unregulated Forex broker list" and you will find updated lists of the companies that are not regulated by recognized authorities and simply act under their own judgment before they get into trouble with their customers, regulators or local authorities. You need to be sure that some legal authority looks over the shoulder of your broker to prevent him from doing something illegal with your money.

Choose a broker that has lower spreads
Well, that's a natural thing to do, right? Yes, but not only because you have better spreads, but because the broker has better dealing banks that offer liquidity for them. It may also mean that the broker is not some bucket shop that does not actually let their customers' orders be opened in the market, but plays against their customers and eventually takes their money. You do want your broker to have better quotes from big banks, because that would mean that those banks trust your broker and so can you.

Consider leverage that is offered

Brokers promote high leverage and often against their customers. They advertise it as a very good thing and it is if you know how to use it and protect yourself from too much risk. Too big leverage can kill your account in no time. I would avoid brokers that offer leverage 1:1000 or even 1:500. The maximum leverage that you can use should not be more than 1:100 and still better 1:50. Anything that goes beyond that is too much. Good brokers want long term clients, not those who are reckless about risk taking and lose their money fast. A good broker will not only take his spreads, but also advise you on using smaller risks.

Can you open an account with a small deposit

This may not mean that a broker is good, but a mini account could be sort of preparation for you to trade real money, but without risking too much. Demo account does not really prepare you to trade live. However, if you risk some 200 or 300 bucks and that is not the amount you cannot afford to lose you can open a mini account and have much better practice than you had by trading a demo account.

Read customer reviews

Although, those might be not entirely reliable you will still find some truth in it. Some companies get a lot of bad reviews and you should avoid such brokers. Do more research about what clients of various brokers are saying and after some time you will get your own impression which brokers might be reliable and which ones should be avoided.

Do they care about their customers?

Most brokers will have customer service. If a broker does not have one, you better avoid him. Those that do not reply to their customer requests within 24 hours should also be avoided. I had an experience when I had to wait for a response from a broker helpline for over a week. That is certainly not the broker I recommend you to go to. No. Go to a broker website, try to use live chat, ask questions and see how they respond. Do not be afraid to ask difficult questions. It is your money at stake, be smart.

So, you see how many points have been covered. After you have gone through all of these points you will probably have some of the issues you will want to analyze too. Do it, better safe than sorry. A good broker is also part of your journey to being a successful trader.

Taking your trading to next level: develop your own trading rules

Having trading rules and following them with discipline is probably the last of essential things that you should have in your trading toolkit. You cannot expect to drift as a ship without direction in the market. You have to know what you are doing and why you are doing it. Otherwise, you will be eaten by the market. Forex is a zero sum game. In order for you to win, somebody has to lose. You can switch the parts. In order for somebody to win, you have to lose. You decide which part you want to take. If you want to be a winner you must have your own trading rules. Let's briefly look at them. Some of them you have heard as they have become slogans, others might be new to you. Anyway, you will surely need them.

Cut your losses short
Newbies hardly ever do that. They keep on expecting that the trade will come back and they will close it with a profit. It often happens, but when it doesn't they can lose half of their account or even all of it. Do not give in to wishful thinking. Cut your losses when they are still small. If your trade is going against you, it means something is not as you have planned and expected and the smartest thing to do is to get out of the market as fast as you can. Do not risk more than 2 percent of your account on any trade.

Let your profits run

Newbies do just the opposite. They let their losses run and cut their profits short. That's why they end up losing it all. The only way you can increase your trading account is by having bigger profits and smaller losses. If you make 100 pips and lose 200 you will soon be finished as a trader. Therefore, you have to make at least double of what you lose in order to be ahead. Trading is not easy and if you take a few pips and run, but let your losses to grow to hundreds of pips you will be finished sooner rather than later. Smart traders let their profits run. They catch a trend and they keep their positions till they outgrow their losses by three, four or even ten times. This is how money can be made in currencies.

Increase your exposure when you are doing well and reduce it when you fail

If you are doing well, you are in touch with the market and can take more risk, or simply open more positions in the direction of the market. This increases your chances to make bigger profits. On the other hand, you have to decrease your exposure to market if you are not doing that well. Trade less, when you have a number of losing trades. You need to have a fresh head, stable emotions and be disciplined when you take a trade. When you feel exhausted or you do not know where the market is going, just don't do anything. You don't have to trade. You have to use opportunities that you see, not the ones you don't see. Loses may force you in a psychological state where you want to recoup losses at any cost. Don't do that. This is a sure way to failure. Stop; let your head cool and only then trade.

Do not overtrade, select your trades

Overtrading is a common "disease" among new traders. They feel they need to be in the market all the time, because they are afraid of missing good trades. The fact is that they pick up a lot of bad trades, which far outweigh the good ones and this leads to never ending losses. If you want to be a good trader who makes money consistently you have to be very selective. Picking random trades will result in mediocre at best and at big losses in most cases.

Don't fight a trend

"Trend is your friend" is an old slogan that most professional Forex traders use. They want to trade in the direction of the prevailing trend and never against it. Money is made when you go with the market flow, not in the opposite direction. Newbies often rely on various indicators that tell them market is overbought or oversold and they start fighting a trend. The fact is that when trends start markets can stay in overbought or oversold territory for a long time. So, do not rely on those indicators and don't fight direction. Better, follow it. Trend trading is by far the easiest and most profitable trading system. Use it to make money.

Be aware of fundamental news releases

A single macroeconomic news release can cause a currency pair to move hundreds of pips in a matter of a few seconds. You do not want to have an open position that goes against you during those market events. Lots of pros simply close their positions before such important news releases as: interest rate decision, Non Farm Payrolls, CPI, General Domestic Product and a few more. Before a week starts, always look at

Economic calendar to see which pieces of news are coming that week and do not trade during those events, only after market calms down and volatility comes back to normal levels.

Understand that market discounts information

Traders know that market participants always look forward. They expect things to happen. Therefore, when some piece of information comes out, it has already been priced in by market participant and market may go in the opposite direction that it is supposed to. Let's say market expects that FED will raise interest rates in half a year's time and the ECB will keep them the same. Now, this expectation pushes eur/usd down till finally the FED starts raising rates. When the news is finally released that interest rates have been increased the market will most likely sell off US dollar as it has already priced in this information.

Have a trading diary

You need to learn from your good and bad trades. Traders who don't learn become losers, because they keep on repeating the same mistakes and those finally cause them to lose everything. You need to monitor your trades, post a chart in your diary with an explanation why you opened a trade. Have some description or explanation as to what motivated you to take that trade. Did you follow your trading rules or you went against them? If it did not work, maybe you can find out why it happened. Have this practice every day and if you do not trade that often, at least once a week. You will see that with time you will make fewer mistakes and take a lot more better trades.

Be a learner

Be a learner. Read books about financial markets, various trading strategies, especially the materials that were published by successful traders. If you learn from them you will become a good trader much faster than you would if you did that all by yourself. You need to understand how good traders think, how they motivate themselves, how they analyze markets and etc. You can model them and eventually join the ranks of those who make consistent money in currencies.

Conclusion

Forex as the largest and most liquid market in the world attracts a lot of new traders who expect to make a fortune, achieve financial freedom and become their own bosses. Unfortunately, very few traders see this come true in their trading careers. Most go bankrupt in a matter of a few months. Is it because the market is only for highly talented or those who have connections? No, everyone can be successful. Anyone who puts enough effort, time and learns from his trading mistakes can become a full time Forex trader.

This eBook has introduced you to basic principles of currency market, taught you about most famous trading strategies and chart patterns that can help you to be successful. It also explained you a few more key elements such as risk management and broker selection that you will need in order to survive in the market. Finally, we dealt with some key rules that every trader should have and keep to with discipline. Those rules will help one to move from a beginner to an intermediate and with enough effort and experience even to advanced level.

You may not become a billionaire or millionaire trading currencies, but if you are persistent, hard learning and not willing to give up you will eventually see that you are able to survive in the market and prosper. Be a learner. Learn from your mistakes. Set new targets and go forward in your career as a trader. Good luck!

Thank you again for purchasing this book!

Thank you and good luck